Also by Anna Pump and Gen LeRoy

Country Weekend Entertaining
The Loaves and Fishes Cookbook

Summer on a Plate

More than 120 Delicious,
No-Fuss Recipes for
Memorable Meals from
Loaves and Fishes

ANNA PUMP AND GEN LeROY

Photography by Alan Richardson

Simon & Schuster
New York   London   Toronto   Sydney

Simon & Schuster
1230 Avenue of the Americas
New York, NY 10020

First Simon & Schuster hardcover edition June 2008

SIMON & SCHUSTER and colophon are registered trademarks of Simon & Schuster, Inc.

For information about special discounts for bulk purchases,
please contact Simon & Schuster Special Sales at
1-800-456-6798 or business@simonandschuster.com.

Designed by Nancy Singer

Manufactured in the United States of America

10   9   8   7   6   5   4   3

Library of Congress Cataloging-in-Publication Data
Pump, Anna.
    Summer on a plate : more than 120 delicious, no-fuss recipes for memorable meals from
Loaves and Fishes / Anna Pump and Gen LeRoy ; photography by Alan Richardson.
    p. cm.
        1. Loaves and Fishes (Store : Sagaponack, N.Y.)
        2. Cookery. 3. LeRoy, Gen. I. Title.
TX652.P92 2008
641.5 dc—22
2007048932

ISBN-13:   978-1-4516-2601-8

For Detlef

Acknowledgments

First and foremost I wish to thank Gen. Without her, there would be no book.

I want to thank my husband, Detlef, whose support, hearty appetite, and encouragement never stopped.

I could not have done this without Sybille van Kempen, my daughter, who is always there with new ideas and who, during the busy summer months, keeps Loaves and Fishes on track. I would also like to thank the entire staff at Loaves and Fishes for their hard work and their unwavering commitment to quality and freshness.

A special thanks to all my loyal customers who, summer after summer, with their praise and gentle critiques, inspire me to come up with new and challenging ideas.

Thanks to our superb editor, Sydny Miner, my agent and friend, Alison Bond, the excellent creative team at Simon & Schuster, Alan Richardson, Jackie Seow, and Michael Pederson, and a special thanks to Alice Mayhew for believing in me.

Finally, a big hug and thanks to all my family for sharing my food while testing and retesting all the recipes and offering their honest critiques—nothing "sugarcoated" as my grandchildren would call it.

—A. P.

Contents

Why This Book?

$\mathcal{I}$t was during one evening last summer, when my friend Alison and I were dining at the Dockside restaurant in Sag Harbor, overlooking the bay with dozens of gleaming boats anchored only a few feet away, that the idea for this book was born. I had been chattering almost nonstop about all the new combinations of tastes and blendings of textures I wanted to try, also about nurturing some newer, fun recipes, about ideas for quick and easy meals, when Alison leaned over and said with a knowing smile, "You're going to write another book, Anna, aren't you?" I couldn't help but smile. Of course! I even had a title ready—*Summer on a Plate*. It had been in the back of my mind for quite a while and now, speaking openly about it, a summer cookbook seemed like the most natural and, to me, most obvious way to offer recipes that I had accumulated over the years, the majority of which were designed especially for the summer season when Loaves and Fishes is open full time.

I wanted to create a cookbook that celebrated summer's glorious bounty from the fields, farms, gardens, and seas. I wanted it to be a book for those of us who adore summertime and summer food and would like to pick up some handy shortcuts for preparing quick, tasty meals in an hour or less from start to finish.

Life should become easier during the summer, when afternoons grow longer and we are able to find peaceful times to lunch on a blanket stretched under a tree, or lie in a hammock while nursing a tall drink, or spend an afternoon picnicking at the beach, or relish those lengthy dusk-to-dark evenings when each sunset is more spectacular than the last. Which brings us to the core of this book: designing easy-to-read, no-fuss, delicious, and memorable meals that will still allow the cook time to enjoy all the pleasures that our summer season has to offer.

Trends in food come and go. People want new ideas, and as soon as any appear they seem to be instantly embraced by anyone who owns a pan. That, to me, is the fun part of creating new recipes; the one thing that has always remained constant is my absolute commitment to good food. I shop and strongly recommend shopping for the finest, top-quality ingredients: my conviction is that all of us should be able to enjoy every kind of food in moderation. It is the principle that lies at the heart of Loaves and Fishes.

Each and every spring, I cannot wait to hang the "Welcome" sign out front of the store, fling open the windows, give the picnic table in back a good scrubbing, and arrange the table in my garden at home in such a way as to catch the dappled sunshine that filters down through the leaves during the day and allows us the fullest view of those moonlit, starry skies at dinner time.

In this book I want to share with you the joy, the thrill of summer cooking. I want to encourage every home cook to take risks, adapt, add to, or subtract from these recipes that are, after all, blueprints for meals that can turn the modest cook into an instant star. That, to me, is the hope behind this book: that you enjoy the recipes as much as I have loved creating them in my heartfelt salute to summer.

How It All Began

It's been twenty-five years since that fateful day when, having heard there was a small cooking store for sale in Sagaponack, Long Island, I drove over and looked it over carefully. A soft natural light spilled in from the bank of windows in front and on one side of the main room, which made the room appear larger than it was. I walked behind the wooden counter and into the kitchen, which seemed to be just the right proportions for someone like me who had catered parties for years, mostly from my own country kitchen in Noyac, sometimes using my customers' kitchens, and many times on outdoor grills under vast tents. The store—already called Loaves and Fishes—was cozy, and I was able to see that its size was certainly manageable. Its embracing atmosphere made me feel immediately at home, and after spending more time inside and then outside in the small, charming garden I decided that I had to buy it.

My husband, Detlef, and I scrubbed the inside from top to bottom, repainted everything white, even the floors, made sure all the facilities were in A-1 condition, weeded the back garden, and planted herbs and vegetables. As we worked, I allowed my imagination to run rampant; new recipes began cluttering my brain, ideas that I had been yearning to test and try but had no space in which to develop were now in almost my every thought. I was, at the same time, excited and terrified. Time flew by at an alarming rate. The season was to begin in approximately two weeks from the time Detlef and I finally mopped our way out the back door. I began buying, storing, planning, baking—I felt as if I had suddenly sprouted eight arms, all of them moving simultaneously. Suddenly, it seemed, opening day was upon us. I had not stopped, filling the shelves with my own freshly baked breads, scones, muffins, pies, and cakes; the cookie jars were gradually filling to their brims, each food bin held new and, I hoped, innovative salads, meats, pastas, grains, and vegetables. Ducks and chickens, crisp and still steaming, were slid off the spits and lined up on a huge wooden tray. Room was made for the savory tarts and the whole roasts, sliced, garnished, and ready to go. Pâtés, dips, dressings, sauces, and hors d'oeuvres were placed in my brand-new freezer and I can't even remember what else, but, believe me, there was more, much more.

When our doors opened, I had been there since before 4:00 a.m., the time when our ovens needed to be turned on for the day's baking. I slipped on a clean and starched white jacket and opened the front door. The shock on my face must have been quite apparent because the first few customers in the line that stretched to the road and curled up its side smiled back at me, and some laughed at my surprised expression. I welcomed everyone inside, and within a few short hours I was putting more ducks and chickens on the spits, whipping up more salads, and taking orders for parties of ten to forty. At around 4:00 p.m. I sat down and treated myself to a cup of strong coffee and a cookie. I felt a glow of extreme pleasure. It had become apparent that this was possibly the beginning of the most exciting, challenging, and demanding part of my life. Looking back at it with today's perspective, it was. And still is.

Summer, for me, begins when the first signs of spring appear, when the earth is launched on its gradual thaw and we can almost sense life beginning to unfold beneath our feet. Windows stay open and breezes begin to usher in intoxicating aromas. Honeybees begin circling fresh flowers or plants that have blossomed overnight. Rows of seedlings in the garden behind Loaves and Fishes begin their greening, and as far as the eye can see, all along the village streets and country roads, plumpish buds are ready to dazzle us with their gorgeous palettes.

It's when April arrives that I begin my early morning ritual of bicycling to the beach. The air is crystal clear, crisp and incredibly invigorating. As I pedal down the hilly road to Main Beach, I pass the seafood shop where our local fishermen, still in their hip-high rubber boots, are delivering crates filled with their catches of the day; seagulls are swirling overhead. I immediately imagine recipes dealing with fish, shrimp, scallops, lobster. I make a mental note to check out what is the freshest and when to expect a delivery to the store.

The air is beginning to warm up as I eventually reach town where the vintage homes are being dressed up for the season; new paint, new cedar shingles, new roofs, flower boxes with baby buds peeking over the rims, trees being pruned, lawns resodded, and behind one house, I can see a young woman scrubbing her grill on the back patio.

I love summer.

Farmers have plowed their fields, potatoes and corn are planted. Outdoor farm stands have begun to display freshly picked young vegetables: baby peas, beans, spinach, white eggplants, greens of all sorts, and baskets overflowing with zucchini, their large, drooping flowers hanging over the edges. What will my customers, many of whom have become close friends over the years, like me to suggest they buy? How should it be prepared? Questions like what reheats well? What is best served chilled? Which foods are safe to bring to the beach? How long does this or that salad, meat, cheese, or vegetable last—these are ones I answer many times each day.

I am delighted to discover fresh goat cheese on sale, local and divine. Green strawberry fields are dotted in red. Hand-painted signs that invite anyone to PICK YOUR OWN remind me of a time, not long ago, when we brought our grandchildren to these annual rituals; their fingers, shirts, and mouths would be stained pink at the end of our outings.

I love preparing food in summer because it's when the freshest produce is so easily accessible and cooking options become limitless. It is my season. The best time to spread my wings, be creative, be inspired, be challenged and like those buds in our flower boxes, I actually feel blessed by the sun and raring to blossom.

Summer on a Plate

Keeping a Step Ahead

What to Buy, How to Store It, What to Freeze

The first rule for preparing no-fuss meals is to have everything you need on hand before you start. All the essential ingredients should be properly stored in your pantry, refrigerator, or freezer. Let's tackle the pantry first.

I know it seems silly to mention salt since it is a common staple used on or in almost everything we eat. I also know that consumer markets and magazines have been bombarded recently with salts of every description and color, harvested from almost every region in the world. For me, kosher salt is and has always been a particular favorite. It has a flakelike texture that allows it to dissolve more easily, has no additives, and with a slightly more pungent taste than ordinary table salt, a pinch goes a long way. Also, if you enjoy a little crunch in your salad that will awaken the taste buds, this is the salt to use.

I'm sure you've been told this many times, but a high-quality imported cold-pressed extra virgin olive oil with a deep, fruity body is a *must*. Safflower, peanut, walnut, canola, and toasted sesame oils should be on your shelves, as well as a bottle of soy sauce. Place a really good aged balsamic vinegar at the top of your list: use it in salad dressings, drizzled on fish, poultry, and in sauces that need a bit of vigor. Rice vinegar, white vinegar, red wine vinegar, and sherry vinegar are all essential to summer cooking and fortunately have very long shelf lives. Preground pepper loses its potency within three to four months, whereas whole peppercorns, stored in a cool, dry place, can last up to a year—the difference between freshly ground and preground pepper is enormous. Other pantry essentials are capers, sesame seeds, red pepper flakes, and mustards—Dijon, in particular. Here's a recipe for a most wonderful and resourceful piquant mustard sauce that you'll find yourself using over and over again.

Grainy Mustard Sauce

      ½ cup grainy mustard

      ½ cup Crème Fraîche (page 30)

      2 tablespoons olive oil

      1 tablespoon honey

      ¼ teaspoon kosher salt

      ¼ teaspoon cayenne pepper

Whisk all the ingredients in a bowl until smooth. Serve at room temperature.

Yields about 1 cup

    ❦ For chicken, add finely chopped fresh basil

    ❦ For lamb, add minced mint leaves

    ❦ For beef, add minced curly parsley or cilantro

Then there are brandy, framboise, and, of course, wines that need to be considered. The wines and alcohol I use in my cooking are ones that I could and would serve to my guests. Don't skimp on any of these items; the better the ingredient, the better your food.

Many recipes call for fresh herbs which, as a rule, are plentiful in the summer, yet I suggest you buy a small supply of dried herbs such as bay leaves, thyme, tarragon, rosemary, mint, dill, oregano, chives, and basil, in case the herbs you want are simply not available. Keep in mind that dried herbs shouldn't be kept for more than six months. Almost every herb can be preserved in oil, and infused oils flavored with individual herbs are an excellent addition to salad dressings, pasta sauces, etc. It's remarkable how quickly the oil absorbs each herb's unique flavor—when you open the bottle the scent is so wonderfully intense.

A tablespoon or two of rosemary oil is great in stews and soups. If you're making fish, try adding a splash of dill or thyme oil. Chive-infused oil is good on about anything raw or cooked. Basil and oregano oils add a gorgeous scent to pasta sauces, sautéed vegetables, and omelets. Depending on your individual tastes, the possibilities are enormous.

Herb–Infused Oil

>　4 loosely packed cups fresh herbs, leaves only, washed and dried
>　2 cups best-quality olive oil

Using a food processor, combine the ingredients and process until the herb is finely minced. Pour the infused oil into a plastic container with a lid. Cover and refrigerate for up to 3 months. Make sure each container is correctly labeled and dated.

Yields about 2½ cups

Fresh basil patches release the most magnificent aromas in summer. When the leaves are puréed with garlic and oil, its concentrated flavor allows a little of it to do its job well. We use our pesto, which is made without cheese, on pastas, in salads, to enrich the flavor of sauces, with fish, chicken—you name it. Here's an easy-as-pie pesto recipe we've been using for years, sometimes substituting walnuts for the pine nuts.

Pesto

> ¼ cup pine nuts
>
> 1½ tablespoons minced garlic
>
> 2½ cups tightly packed basil leaves
>
> ¾ cup olive oil
>
> ½ teaspoon kosher salt
>
> ½ teaspoon freshly ground black pepper

Process the pine nuts and garlic in a food processor for 30 seconds, until well combined. Add the basil, oil, salt, and pepper and purée until smooth.

Yields 1¼ cups

❋ Double or triple the ingredients and freeze in ice cube trays. When set, remove the pesto cubes from the trays and store in a resealable plastic bag. Use the individual cubes as additions to sauces, dips, or dressings. Or freeze in 1-cup plastic containers for larger needs. Frozen, it lasts forever. Covered and refrigerated, it lasts up to 3 months.

Buy the best quality spices: cinnamon, allspice, cloves, ground white pepper, cayenne pepper, sage, saffron, and curry powder. Really good curry is a creation of many spices, such as coriander, turmeric, fenugreek, cumin, cayenne pepper, ginger, allspice, and nutmeg. We mustn't forget the unique and costly saffron that is a requisite for many European and Middle Eastern dishes. Don't get powdered saffron—you never know if or how it's been adulterated. Best to buy a few threads of saffron that, when stored in an airtight container and kept in a cool dark place, will last up to six months. It's a colorful, pungent, aromatic spice that brightens all sorts of rice dishes, risottos, and, of course, bouillabaisse.

If you bake, almond extract is a good idea—and of course vanilla extract. Get the real thing; it may be more expensive but it's worth it. If you're making custards, chantilly cream, pie fillings, cakes, cookies, or almost any kind of pudding, the recipe will most likely require a teaspoon or so of vanilla. Here's a wonderful recipe that is so easy and lasts forever.

Vanilla Beans in Vodka

> 12 whole vanilla beans (I use Madagascar beans)
> 3 cups vodka

Stand the vanilla beans in a tall jar with a tight-fitting lid. Pour in enough vodka to entirely cover the beans. Put the lid in place and store at room temperature for three weeks, allowing the beans to soften. Use the liquid as you would any commercial extract; simply make sure the vanilla beans are always fully immersed in vodka.

> ❦ For a special flavor, remove a bean from the vodka, cut off the tip, and squeeze some essence into your recipe—your guests will notice the taste instantly. Return the same bean to the vodka and it will continue flavoring the extract.

Yields 3 cups

Keeping a step ahead can be as simple as adding mint leaves or slivers of lemon or lime to each compartment of your ice cube trays. After the ice is frozen, seal the cubes in plastic bags. It's a delightful way to dress up tall glasses of iced tea, seltzer water, or just about any mixed cocktail.

Toss some walnuts, pecans, almonds, pine nuts, and hazelnuts into your shopping cart; when you get home, seal them in plastic bags and freeze them. Nuts will last much longer when stored this way. Bread crumbs, too, ought to be sealed and stored in the freezer.

You will need raisins, shredded coconut, and dried cherries, all to be kept inside airtight containers. Don't forget that unbleached all-purpose flour, whole-wheat flour, panko bread crumbs, cornmeal, wild rice, couscous, wheat berries, and plain rice should also be stored inside airtight jars.

The use of salt in commercial butter is to preserve its shelf life. To control the amounts in our recipes, we only use unsalted butter. I love its taste and freshness. If you wish to use unsalted butter (and I do recommend it) and your intent is not to use it all within one week, then store it in your freezer, which is what I do.

Many recipes call for sautéing with clarified butter. Because it has no milk residue, clarified butter won't burn when cooked over high temperatures. Here's what you do:

Clarified Butter

Melt 16 tablespoons (8 ounces) unsalted butter over low heat. Do not allow it to boil. Skim the foam off the top. Pour the clear butter into a crock or clean jar, leaving any milky residue at the bottom of the pan to be discarded. Cover and refrigerate for up to 3 weeks.

Yields ¾ cup (12 tablespoons), but can easily be doubled

I suggest you make and freeze uncooked pie shells. When ready to use, unwrap the shell, fill it, and bake it. Once you've accomplished this easy task and reaped the benefits, you'll be making these pie shells throughout the year. This amazingly simple recipe can be used for dessert pies or savory tarts.

Pie or Tart Shells

> 4 cups unbleached all-purpose flour
> 12 tablespoons (6 ounces) cold unsalted butter, cut into small pieces
> 12 tablespoons (6 ounces) cold margarine, cut into small pieces
> ½ cup plus 2 tablespoons cold water

Place the flour, butter, and margarine in a food processor fitted with a metal blade. Pulse 5 or 6 times until the mixture becomes crumbly. With the motor running, add the water all at once and process until the dough starts to cling together. Turn the dough onto a lightly floured surface, gather it into a ball, flatten the ball into a disk, wrap it in plastic, and refrigerate the dough for 30 minutes.

Unwrap the dough and cut the disk into four equal pieces. Working on a lightly floured surface, roll out each piece into ⅛-inch-thick rounds. Fit each round into its own 9-inch pie dish or tart pan. Carefully wrap each shell in foil, label, and freeze.

When ready to use, discard the foil and assemble the tart or pie with your favorite filling. The crust will be much crisper when baked this way.

Yields 4 crusts